MW00964124

A FRIEND
SHOULD BE
A MAGICIAN,
A PHYSICIAN,
BUT MOSTLY
FOND O' FISHIN'

A FRIEND SHOULD BE A MAGICIAN, A PHYSICIAN, BUT MOSTLY FOND O' FISHIN'

BILLY SPRAGUE

ILLUSTRATIONS BY DENNAS DAVIS

WOLGEMUTH & HYATT, PUBLISHERS, INC.
BRENTWOOD, TENNESSEE

© 1990 by Billy Sprague. All rights reserved.
Published November 1990. First Edition.
Printed in the United States of America.
97 96 95 94 93 92 91 90   8 7 6 5 4 3 2 1

Illustrations © by Dennas Davis. All rights reserved.

No part of this publication may be reproduced, stored in
a retrieval system, or transmitted in any form by any
means, electronic, mechanical, photocopy, recording, or
otherwise, without the prior written permission of
publisher, except for brief quotations in critical reviews
or articles.

Wolgemuth & Hyatt, Publishers, Inc.
1749 Mallory Lane, Suite 110
Brentwood, Tennessee 37027

To My faithful
amie pour la vie,
Anita McAlister

A FRIEND
SHOULD BE
A MAGICIAN

HE SHOULD
SUDDENLY APPEAR
WHEN YOU
NEED HIM

TURN A FROWN
INTO A SMILE
WHEN
YOU SEE HIM

AND
PROVE THERE'S
MORE
THAN YOU CAN
SEE
TO BELIEVE IN

AND A
FRIEND
SHOULD BE
A
PHYSICIAN

HE SHOULD
REMOVE
YOUR
DISCONTENT

STITCH UP
YOUR
PREDICAMENT

AND
ACCEPT
ONLY LOYALTY
AS PAYMENT

BUT
MOST OF
ALL...

A FRIEND
SHOULD BE
FOND O'
FISHIN'

HE SHOULD
WAIT
FOR YOU
PATIENTLY

BAIT YOU
WITH
COUTH

LURE
YOU WITH
HONESTY

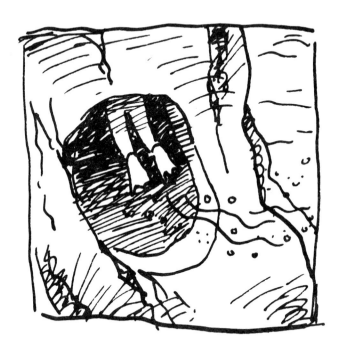

HOOK YOU
ON
TRUTH

HE SHOULD
PULL YOU
IN
FIRMLY

LAND
YOU ON
SHORE

THEN RELEASE
YOU TO BE
WHAT
YOU WERE
CREATED
FOR